William Bolcom/Arnold Weinstein

MINICABS

minicabaret songs

for medium/low voice and piano

ISBN 978-1-4234-7543-9

EDWARD B. MARKS MUSIC COMPANY

EXCLUSIVELY DISTRIBUTED BY

HAL•LEONARD®
CORPORATION

7777 W. BLUEMOUND RD. P.O. BOX 13819 MILWAUKEE, WI 53213

www.ebmarks.com
www.halleonard.com

1. I Feel Good
I feel good about something
and I'm going to find out what it is!

2. People Change
People change
into what they are.

3. Those
Those who want to all the time
do it less than those who don't.

4. Food Song #1
Are you anti-pasto
or pro-volone?

5. Food Song #2
French food — flambé.
Mexican food — olé.
Jewish food — oy vay.

6. I Will Never Forgive You
I will never forgive you
for my behavior.

7. Songette
You lie through your teeth!
but one little tooth says,
"How can you lie?
You don't know the truth."

8. Not Even a Haiku
I rub your name.
My life appears.

9. Maxim #1
Half started, half begun.

10. Maxim #2
You can whack a baby's behind
with a dead turkey but
don't spill tomato aspic
on the Law!

11. Anyone
Anyone who cares enough about you
to steal your mail can't be all bad.

12. Finale: Mystery of the Song?
Mystery of the song?
It means what it means
and you mean what you mean
and how the two do together
spells the song.

NOTE: Inspired in part by Carrie Jacobs Bond's *Half-Minute Songs*, these "minicabs" — mini-cabaret songs — are fashioned from sometimes one-line sketches in Arnold Weinstein's papers, at other times certain phrases that had been unsuccessfully kited from show to opera to play without ever previously finding homes. **WB**

CONTENTS

MINICABS
minicabaret songs
1. I Feel Good

ARNOLD WEINSTEIN

WILLIAM BOLCOM

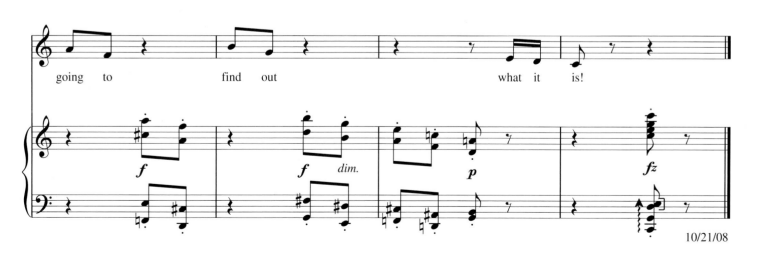

10/21/08

2

2. People Change

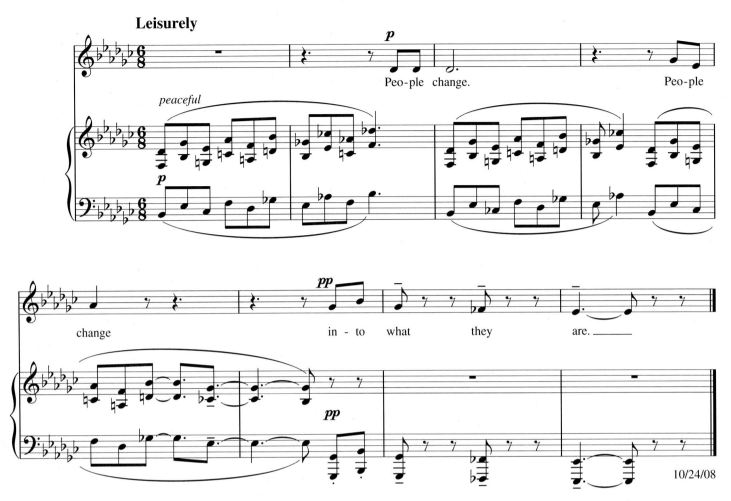

3. Those

4. Food Song #1

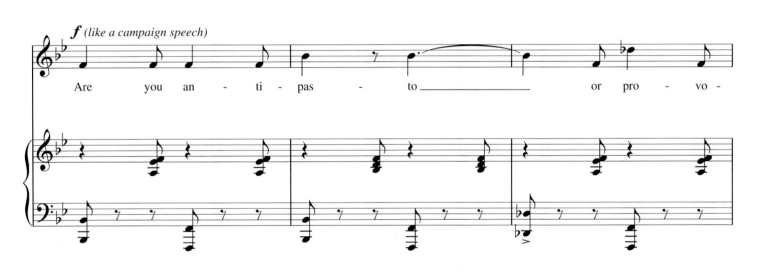

Are you an - ti - pas - to _____ or pro - vo -

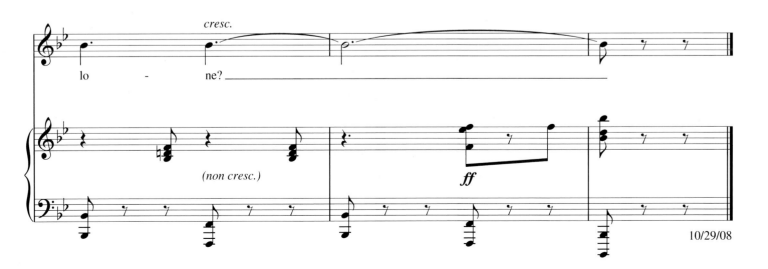

lo - ne? _____

5. Food Song #2

Languorous Waltz

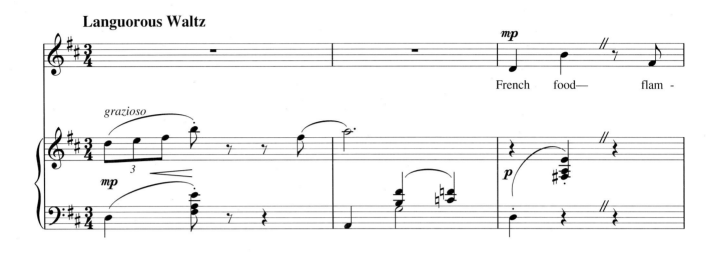

French food— flam -

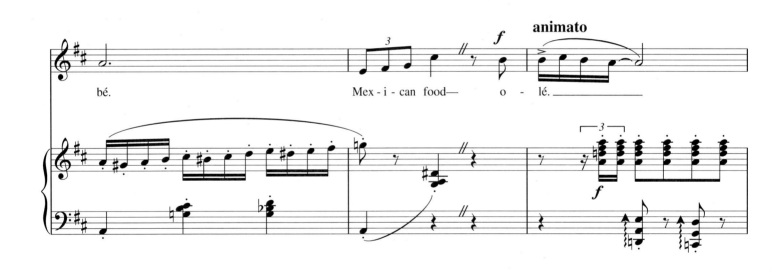

bé.   Mex - i - can food— o - lé. _____

Tempo I   **a little slower**   **rit.**

Jew - ish food—   oy   vay.

10/29/08

6. I Will Never Forgive You

I will nev-er for-give you!   Nev-er   for-give you

for   my   be - hav - ior.

11/2/08

6

7. Songette

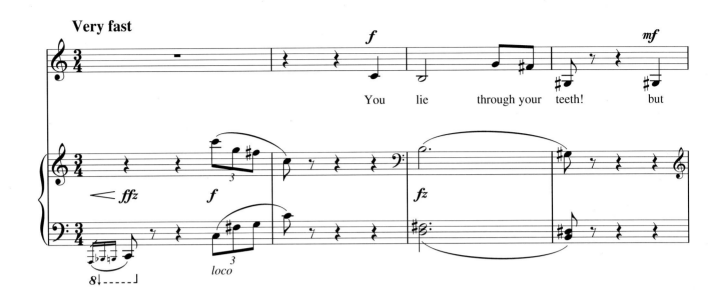

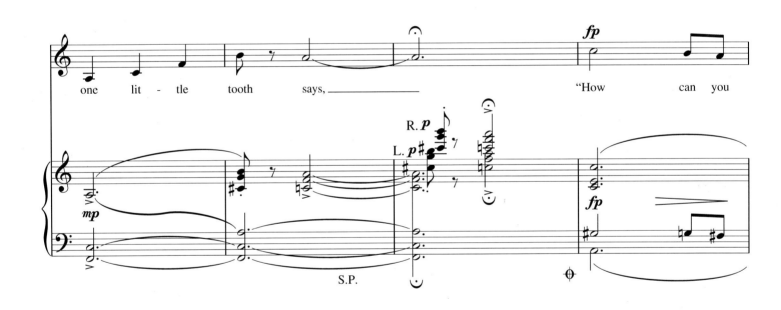

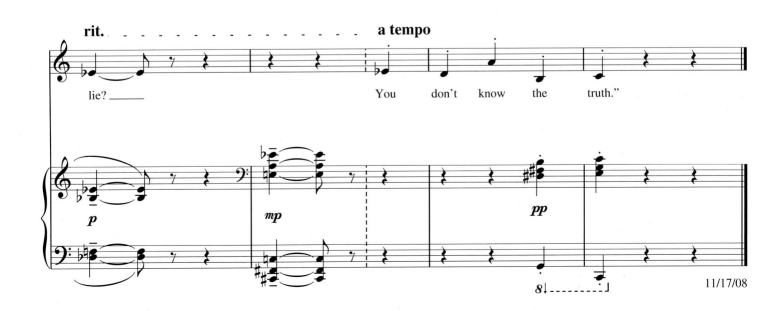

11/17/08

8. Not Even a Haiku

Very slow

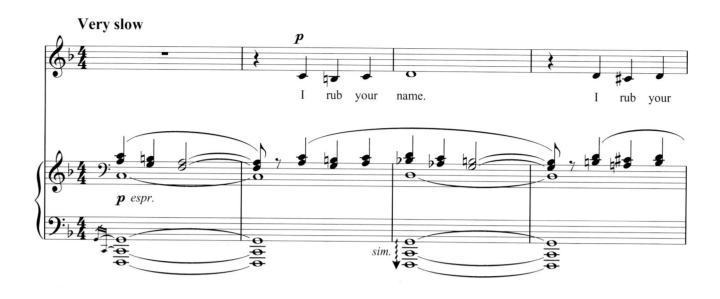

I rub your name. I rub your

name. _____ My life, _____ my

life ap - pears. _____

10/29/08
revised 11/3/08

hommage à C.J.B.
9. Maxim #1

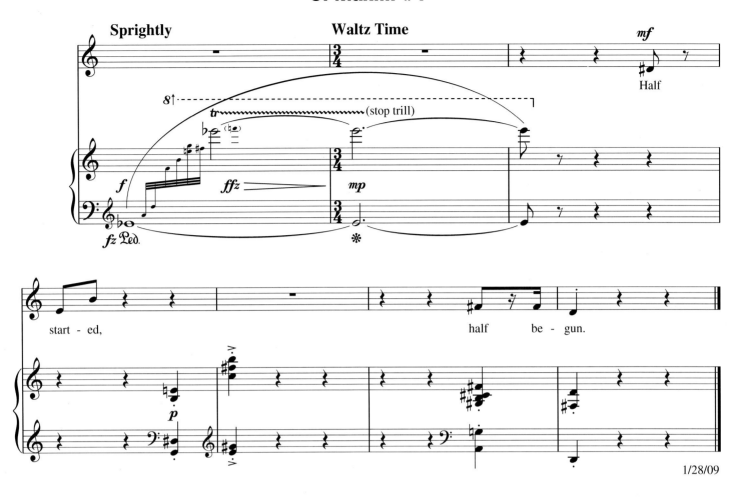

1/28/09

10. Maxim #2

as - pic ___   on the Law! ___

11/18/08

11. Anyone

An - y - one

who cares e - nough a - bout you ___ to steal your mail ___

___ can't ___ be all ___ bad. ___

5/17/09

12. Finale: Mystery of the Song?

Mys - ter - y _____ of the song? _____

It means what it means and you mean what you mean _____ and how the two do to-geth - er _____ spells the song.

5/18/09
Ann Arbor, Mich.